Money or Maker

Studies for individuals
and small groups

Mark Lloydbottom

Copyright @2016 by Your Money Counts

All rights reserved.

Published by Your Money Counts, UK.

Unless otherwise noted, Scripture quotations are from the Holy Bible:

New International Version – UK, Copyright © 1973, 1978, 1984 by the International Bible Society.

Verses identified as NLT are taken from the Holy Bible: New Living Translation, Copyright © 1996, 2004 by Tyndale Charitable Trust. Used by permission of Tyndale House Publishers.

Verses identified as KJV are taken from the King James Version of the Bible: Public Domain.

Verses identified as TLB are taken from The Living Bible, Copyright © 1973 by the Zondervan Corporation.

ISBN: 978-1-908423-17-7

Printed in the United Kingdom

Design: Dickie Dwyer

Layout: Loulita Gill

Welcome

We are so thankful that you have decided to commit to this Money or Maker individual/small group study. The Lord has used the principles you are about to study in the lives of millions of people around the world.

How we view God determines how we live. God owns all our possessions. As a consequence if we are to be committed followers of Christ we must recognise His ownership and allow Him to become the Lord of our money and possessions. God is our provider and Lord of the universe. We are to handle our money faithfully and be good stewards.

Money or Maker comprises five short studies covering the essential pillars of biblical finance. In order to gain a deeper understanding of what the Bible teaches we strongly recommend that you read Bought which can be ordered via the website yourmoneycounts.org.uk. Each study recommends reading one part of Bought.

Each study starts with a suggested aligned Bible memory verse. This will help you remember the important principles.

If you are studying this in a small group you will be able to participate in the 'viewpoint' discussion sessions while if you are studying alone these will provide an opportunity to think and reflect on how you feel the biblical principles apply to you.

Your small group leader may suggest you read the commentary notes for the next study meeting so that you are familiar with the content and focus.

Again, we are thankful for your commitment to this study and pray that the Lord will bless you in every way as you learn His way of handling money and possessions.

Mark Lloydbottom

Your Money Counts
www.yourmoneycounts.org.uk

Your Money Counts is a UK registered charity and is associated globally with Compass – finances God's way.

"No one can serve two masters. Either you will hate the one and love the other, or you will be devoted to the one and despise the other. You cannot serve both God and money."

Matthew 6:24

Table of contents

7	Study 1	Getting started
23	Study 2	The Bible: a blueprint for living
39	Study 3	Free to serve Him
55	Study 4	Growing in generosity
69	Study 5	Save. Invest. Spend.

The handling of money is one aspect of life that most of us think about every day. Some have enough to satisfy their wants. Others never seem to have enough – sometimes there is too much month at the end of the money!

Some struggle to work out how much money is enough. Newspapers…media…social media…the internet. There is no shortage of those wishing to impart their wisdom.

The Bible also has a lot to say about money and possessions and for Christians that has to be a great place to start seeking guidance and good counsel.

We trust that as you get started on this journey of five studies that you will be blessed and encouraged that the Lord desires that we understand His guidelines for ensuring that finances are not mishandled. Or, if you are challenged in this area that you can connect your faith with your situation and find a path to financial freedom.

———

Getting started

1

SCRIPTURE MEMORY VERSE

"Everything in the heavens and earth is yours, O Lord, and this is your kingdom. We adore you as being in control of everything. Riches and honour come from you alone, and you are the ruler of all mankind; your hand controls power and might, and it is at your discretion that men are made great and given strength."

1 Chronicles 29:11-12, (TLB)

BOUGHT

We recommend that before each study you read a few chapters of Bought. The relevant part for this study is: Part 1: An introduction: Issues and problems.

Watch the short video Bought.
This can be downloaded
by following the links on the website -
yourmoneycounts.org.uk/video-intro.

INTRODUCTION

A study guide on finance? Your first reaction might be one of apprehension or even maybe uncertainty as to how studying finance fits into the scope of the church's teaching – apart from giving of course! Yet, everyone else 'out there' has a view on money – usually how to spend or invest it. The media find opportunities to air their views on the subject of finance whether it is about a financial crisis, government or personal debt, payday lender rates of interest or pensions. The world's economy so often prevails in our minds or at least it is the financial challenges that we so often hear about that we perhaps prefer not to concern ourselves about – unless of course there is something that directly concerns us.

So, with all of the focus that finances so often receive, is there anything that we need to know as Christians that emanates from our faith and trust in God? The answer as you may expect from a biblical study on finances is 'yes.' This may well be the first time you have specifically studied what the Bible has to say about the handling of money and possessions. So let us first of all establish why this study is important.

THE BIBLE IS BIG ON INSTRUCTION

In the Bible's 66 books there are 31,102 verses and 2,350 of them are about the handling of money and possessions - that is more than on prayer and faith combined. In fact there are more verses on the handling of money and possessions than on any other subject apart from God himself. To find out more visit the yourmoneycounts.org.uk website and download your free copy of Foundation Truth – this lists all the 2350 verses.

More than 15 per cent of Jesus' recorded words were on this subject and more than half of the parables revolve around the handling of money and possessions.

WHY?

God's economy is very different from man's economy. We may have absorbed through life's journey how man's economy works but

NOTES

NOTES

as those who love the Lord Jesus do we know how our faith impacts in how we handle money?

OUR RELATIONSHIP WITH GOD

Our prayer life partly determines our relationship with the Lord. As does our Bible study, fellowship with other Christians and also our handling of money and possessions.

Q: How do you feel about the weight of Scripture that is devoted to the handling of our money and possessions?

GAINING PERSPECTIVE

As we start on the journey to uncover how God's economy works remember that while man's economy has some very serious fault lines God's economy has never and will never fail. But the Bible is not written by topic so we will navigate around the books and chapters as we start to piece together the jigsaw of God's economic plan for the handling of money and possessions.

Our daily lives are interwoven with decisions about the handling of money and possessions. In fact money is probably one of those matters that you think about at some point every day. Those with enough or more than enough have just as many challenges as those who do not. Never before have there been so many opportunities to spend and sometimes the money we spend is not ours – it is borrowed. For some, their wealth defines them – their car, house, clothes and jewellery. For Christians it is our faith that defines us although we seemingly inevitably conform in so many ways to the 'ways of the world' (Romans 12:2).

The Bible wonderfully reveals God's plans. Romans 5:8 tells us about God's plan to send Jesus to save us from our sins and provide a pathway to eternity.

The Bible can teach us so much of what we need to know for leading life today (2 Peter 1:3). We are called to live lives of godliness. For example in our social interactions, with employers, employees and customers, in our homes with family, and most importantly in the handling of money and possessions.

Jesus said that, "Where our treasure is there your heart will be also," (Matthew 6:21). Where your money goes is a clear sign as to where your heart and mind are. What we do with our money is an indicator of what the Lord means to us. Our heart follows that which we treasure as well as that which we desire and what our eyes see. What does the Bible have to say about the eyes and the heart? The answer is found in Ephesians 1:18, "I pray that the eyes of your heart may be enlightened in order that you may know the hope to which he has called you, the riches of his glorious inheritance in his holy people." The Bible and our prayer life turn our hearts toward the Lord. Remember that what we think about determines what we see in our eyes and that in turn drives what we do.

Can we serve two masters? Maybe you might think that is possible but the Bible enlightens us otherwise. Paul cannot make it any clearer when he writes in Matthew 6:24, "No one can serve two masters. Either you will hate the one and love the other, or you will be devoted to the one and despise the other. You cannot serve both God and Money." So, where do you find your deepest joy – in Christ or your possessions? Few can perhaps say Christ without thinking about the material possessions? But that is largely in the western world. Less than 15 hours by plane there are those who have very little – to eat or wear. And that is even true of some in this country. For further study read the account of the rich man and Lazarus in Luke 16:19-31 and especially verse 25.

Q: How can we incorporate God's Word into our financial plans? Read Proverbs 7:2; Ephesians 5:17 and Joshua 1:8

THE LORD IS OUR PROVIDER

READ MATTHEW 6:33, AND 1 KINGS 17:4,6

God led the Israelites for 40 years, satisfied the hunger of the 4,000 and 5,000 men. How will God meet our needs? We cannot always know but He is faithful to His promises (Philippians 4:19). But it is important to distinguish between wants and needs. Needs

NOTES

are necessities and are defined by Paul as shelter, food and clothing. Wants are anything over and above. The key is prayer, patience and holding onto your faith. For we serve a God who has no limits as Jeremiah tells us in 32:17, "Lord, you have made the heavens and the earth by your great power and outstretched arm. Nothing is too hard for you."

Take hold of what we can learn from the Bible concerning money and possessions and enjoy the freedom that comes from following our Maker's economy. We are called to live life with an eternal perspective and when we apply what we learn from the Bible to our income and spending decisions then we can draw away from the pull of modern culture and materialism. Maybe the lures of man's economy to 'buy this because you deserve it' won't be quite so great, tempting or overwhelming. Enjoy discovering how God wants us to act, draw closer to Him and set aside the anxieties that money problems so often bring.

GOD'S PART

The Lord did not design people to shoulder the responsibilities that only He can carry. Jesus said "Come to Me, all who are weary and heavy-laden, and I will give you rest. Take My yoke upon you…. For My yoke is easy and My burden is light" (Matthew 11:28-30), Come to Me! God has assumed the burdens of ownership, control, and provision. For this reason, His yoke is easy and we can rest and enjoy the peace of God – if we only will.

For many, the primary challenge is failing to consistently recognise God's part. Our culture believes that God plays no part in financial matters, and we have, in some measure, been influenced by that view.

Another reason for this is that God has chosen to be invisible. Anything that is "out of sight" tends to become "out of mind." We get out of the habit of recognising His ownership, control, and provision.

OUR PART

Complete this study to find out what the Bible says about our part.

 BIBLE ASPECTS

Read and consider what you can learn from...

1. Luke 16:11-15
What are the true riches? Who do we serve?

2. Isaiah 55:8-9
How different is our perspective from God's

3. 1 Timothy 6:10
How can we avoid falling into this trap?

4. 1 Timothy 5:8
We are instructed to... or else...

5. 1 Chronicles 29:11-12
It's mine. My house. My car. Is it?

NOTES

6. **Romans 12:2**

What does it mean to not be conformed in the context of money and possessions?

7. **Mark 8:36**

What is the warning and in the context of the handling of money the practical application?

8. **Luke 12:15-21**

Where our money goes is like a barometer of what God means to us.

 **VIEW POINT**

1. What was new to you?
2. What was of most interest from this first study?
3. What is God's role in your income and possessions?
4. What are your areas of influence and authority with regards money and possession – do these coincide with what we have studied thus far?
5. Money is a primary competitor with Christ for our affection. Are you allowing Him to lead your financial life and if so what does it look like?

6. From the list below discuss the pulls of our culture and how this can be changed?
   a. Possessions bring happiness
   b. What we own defines us
   c. Having what you want now is important

 ACTION STATIONS

1. Where do you see that you might need to change your understanding about handling of your finances.

2. Pray about those areas where He doesn't have control of your spending.

3. Commit to not missing any of these studies.

 BACK TO THE BIBLE

Here are a few additional verses that will help to deepen your understanding of what the Bible has to say about finances.

Genesis 1:1

Psalm 24:1

Deuteronomy 8:17-18

Haggai 2:8

Leviticus 25:23

NOTES

MAN'S WISDOM

Where riches hold dominion of the heart God has lost his authority.

John Calvin

If a person gets his attitude toward money straight, it will straighten out almost every other area of life.

Billy Graham

The Word of God well understood and religiously obeyed is the shortest route to spiritual perfection. And we must not select a few favourite passages to the exclusion of others. Nothing less than a whole Bible can make a whole Christian.

A W Tozer

LOOKING FORWARD

Our next study develops in more depth some of the aspects included in this study. Look ahead and read the Bible verses so that you come fully prepared to be involved in the group discussions.

Think and pray about those areas of your life that you sense now need to come under the Lordship of Christ.

Revisit this study and ask the Lord to help you apply what you have learnt.

Extra time
———

GET MORE INSIGHTS AT
→ WWW.YOURMONEYCOUNTS.ORG.UK

NOTES

 ### JOIN US AT THE COFFEE SHOP

Visit www.yourmoneycounts.org.uk/resources for a further opportunity to view the coffee shop discussions related to this study.

 ### DO YOU NEED TO COMPLETE THIS STUDY?

It may be that your group did not complete this study. Why not review this study again before you next meet? There are some really important principles and personal study provides a great opportunity to weigh and pray what you have learnt and how this might apply to you.

 ### GOING DEEPER

After each study we include some additional verses or thoughts that you might wish to study to add further understanding to differing aspects of managing finance and possessions God's way.

Here are some further verses to look up and an invitation to learn the Scripture memory verse prior to the next study.

WHAT THE BIBLE SAYS ABOUT POSSESSIONS

Genesis 14:12	Can entice and enslave us
Exodus 20:17	How you can envy them
Isaiah 3:16-26	Don't abuse yours
Haggai 1:6	Why they don't satisfy
Matthew 6:24	Do yours possess you?
Matthew 19:16-22	Should believers give theirs away?

Mark 10:21	Are you willing to give them up?
Luke 16:19-31	Being selfish with
Acts 2:44	Are you willing to share yours with others?
Acts 20:33	How to be satisfied with what you have
James 2:2-4	Why do we attribute such importance to?
Revelation 3:17	Can cause indifference to your faith

 ## MATERIALISM QUIZ

1. Do you find yourself setting your goals based on achieving a certain financial status or accumulating certain possessions (house, car etc)?
2. Do you almost never seem to have enough time for your family because you have to spend so much time at work?
3. Do you find yourself saying "If I could just get to this point financially, I would be satisfied and happy?"
4. Do you find yourself getting into unneeded debt trying to compete with your friends?

Read Ecclesiastes 5:10-14

"Whoever loves money never has enough; whoever loves wealth is never satisfied with their income. This too is meaningless. As goods increase, so do those who consume them. And what benefit are they to the owners except to feast their eyes on them? The sleep of a labourer is sweet, whether they eat little or much, but as for the rich, their abundance permits them no sleep. I have seen a grievous evil under the sun: wealth hoarded to the harm of its owners, or wealth lost through some misfortune, so that when they have children there is nothing left for them to inherit."

NOTES

Q: What do you think these verses say about a person who is materialistic?

The Bible tells us that contentment is being satisfied with where we are and what we have because of who we are in Christ.

Society says: "God plays no role in handling money, and my happiness is based on my being able to afford my standard of living."

But, it is impossible to be truly satisfied with material possessions. We will always want more and always be disappointed because the material possessions that we attain don't bring the satisfaction that we thought they would. That is because God is the only one that can give us lasting satisfaction and contentment.

 ## SCRIPTURE MEMORY VERSE

A verse to commit to memory before the next study...

"If you have not been trustworthy in handling worldly wealth, who will trust you with true riches?"

(Luke 16:11)

 ## YOUR THOUGHTS, REFLECTIONS, COMMITMENTS AND ACTIONS

"But you shall remember the Lord your God, for it is He who is giving you power to make wealth, that He may confirm His covenant which He swore to your fathers, as it is this day."

Deuteronomy 8:18

We are called to be faithful managers. That is not easy in a society that is materialistic and encourages the acquisition of possessions, which can compromise our ability to be faithful in our service of Him and others. We are called to live a life with an eternal perspective and for our hearts and minds to be transformed.

A baby soon gets to grip with ownership – especially when there is an older sibling around. But we also need to beware as we are also conditioned to think of possessions as 'mine.'

We trust that this foundational study will be a real blessing as you work through the implications of God's ownership in your life.
───────

A blueprint for living

2

SCRIPTURE MEMORY VERSE

"If you have not been trustworthy in handling worldly wealth, who will trust you with true riches?"

Luke 16:11

BOUGHT

We recommend that before the next study you read a few chapters of Bought. The relevant part for this study is:
Part 2: The Bible: A blueprint for living.
You may also wish to visit:
www.yourmoneycounts.org.uk/blueprint-for-living.

INTRODUCTION

In Getting Started we learnt that the Bible has a lot to say about the handling of our money and possessions. We started to consider how man's economy differs from God's economy. We looked at the importance of not being conformed to the ways of the world; rather being transformed by the renewing of our minds. How this applies to the handling of our money and possessions is important. Are you willing to align your actions more closely with the Bible's instruction?

Q: How would you summarise what you learnt from Getting Started?

These studies go to the heart of aspects of our day to day living that can be challenging.

HELP IS AT HAND – HERE IS THE PSALMIST'S PRAYER:

"Help me to prefer obedience to making money! Turn me away from wanting any other plan than yours. Revive my heart toward you. Reassure me that your promises are for me, for I trust and revere you" (Psalm 119, 36-38 (TLB).

OWNERSHIP

1 Corinthians 10:26 repeats what we read in Psalm 24:1, "The earth is the Lord's, and everything in it."

The Lord is the owner of everything. He made it all – the silver and the gold, the cattle on a thousand hills - and the hills themselves (Psalm 50:10).

"It's mine" is often how we look at those possessions we have bought. A young child certainly understands all about ownership. How long before a child cries when something is taken from them. Maybe an older sibling borrows a toy only for the younger to remonstrate and cry out "it's mine"? We might be prepared to lend something but we mostly expect it to be returned and in the same state when lent. Yes, we understand ownership and know that it is a belief system that is not easy to move away from. But with the Lord's help – anything is possible.

SO, IF GOD OWNS EVERYTHING WHAT DOES THAT MAKE US?

The Bible has an answer to that question in that it tells us that we are a steward - or manager could be another word to describe our relationship to what we 'own.' This is just about the toughest change in mind-set because it most likely challenges the language and view we have taken all our lives with regard to 'stuff.' Let's look at what stewardship is and what it entails.

STEWARDSHIP

A steward is a manager of someone else's possessions and the Lord gives us the authority to be stewards, "You made them rulers over the works of your hands; you put everything under their feet" Psalm 8:6.

And the Lord requires that we be faithful stewards. In Luke 16:11 we read "If you have not been trustworthy in handling worldly wealth, who will trust you with true riches" Faithful use of worldly wealth leads us to the true riches. If we handle money and possessions according to the principles of Scripture our fellowship with Christ will grow stronger. However if we manage our money and possessions unfaithfully, our fellowship with Christ will suffer.

When we think of using our money to impact the world for Christ, we often think of giving money to the church or supporting someone going on a mission trip. Those things are important but the most important thing to recognise is that financial obedience brings intimacy with the Lord. Even more than our money, God wants our heart. When our heart is fully devoted to the Lord in the area of our finances, then He can use the finances He has given us to impact the world. But it is not about impacting the world, it's about Jesus impacting the world through us.

GAINING PERSPECTIVE

Our responsibility as stewards is clearly stated by Paul in 1 Corinthians 4:2, "it is required that those who have been given a trust must prove faithful."

Be faithful with what we have been given. The Bible gives us an understanding about stewardship when we study the parable of the talents (money) in Matthew 25:14-30. The owner praised the two who had doubled what they had been given while reprimanding the one who had buried his talent. The key lesson here is that we should be faithful in using that which we have been given – no matter how great or small. That does not just apply to money but in all areas of that which we have been given.

The Lord desires to have an intimate relationship with us and possessions can get in the way. Think – television, notebooks, the Internet, sport and so on. How much time do we spend using or watching those things that we have acquired compared to time in prayer or Bible study?

Q: Do you really believe that you are accountable to God as to how you have managed His money and possessions that have been entrusted to you? Luke 12:42-48.

BIBLE ASPECTS

Read and consider what you can learn from...

1. **Matthew 25:21**
What does the faithful steward enjoy?

2. **2 Corinthians 9:10**
What does the Lord provide?

NOTES

3. **Malachi 3:10**
What is the Lord's invitation?

4. **2 Corinthians 9:11**
What is the law of the harvest?

5. **Luke 16:10-12**
What does the Bible tell us about trust?

PROVISION

How are you feeling at this point in our study? Positive or maybe a little apprehensive? Uncertain as to what this might mean for the way you handle your finances? Let's be clear – this is all good news, well it would be as it is all from God's Word and He only has our best interests at heart and our close relationship with Him. Remember we have a jealous God and He wants us to love Him. So does being a steward have any adverse consequences? Will you be able to provide for your needs?

Matthew instructs us to, "seek first his kingdom and his righteousness, and all these things will be given to you as well" (Matthew 6:33). But the first part is clear in that we are to seek first His kingdom and His righteousness (being right in God's sight). These are some of the most popular and challenging words in all of the New Testament. This is Jesus' practical antidote to worry: Set your mind on other things than the length of life, food to eat and clothes to wear.

What does it mean to seek first? A kingdom in which He is the undisputed Lord, where all things are His, where the final word is His, where the highest purposes are His. Christians understand this and submit to it. What would Jesus do? Is perhaps a very helpful question to drive this idea. Jesus, Lord in my home, Lord of my friendships, Lord of my career and family. Lord of my financial activities and Lord of all my plans and initiatives.

He is our provider. The same Lord who fed manna to the children of Israel after they had fled Egypt. The same Lord who fed thousands from two small loaves and two fishes. The same Lord who said to Elijah, "You will drink from the brook, and I have instructed the ravens to supply you with food there.' The ravens brought him bread and meat in the morning and bread and meat in the evening, and he drank from the brook" (1 Kings 17:4,6).

God is both predictable and unpredictable. Totally predictable in His faithfulness to provide for our needs. What we cannot predict is how the Lord will provide. One key to understanding how the Lord provides is to take hold of the importance of being content.

Q: How has the Lord provided for you when you were in need?

CONTENTMENT

Paul writes, "I have learned to be content whatever the circumstances. I know what it is to be in need, and I know what it is to have plenty. I have learned the secret of being content in any and every situation, whether well fed or hungry, whether living in plenty or in want" (Philippians 4:11-12). And in Hebrews 13:5, "Keep your lives free from the love of money and be content with what you have."

There is no doubt that being content is integrally linked to our provision. The challenge we can face is that there is so much 'stuff' to buy. Having the latest phone. Changing the car. Buying new clothes. Going away somewhere warm and exotic. While at school, children see what others have and don't wish to be left out. Visit the supermarket and temptation sits on the shelves. "Can I have...?"

NOTES

NOTES

Every advert has as its goal an intention to make you discontent. How many advertising messages do we see each day? If we include all those banner ads it is probably somewhere in the region of 300-700. Not so sure they had that particular challenge when the Bible was written!

AVOID THE EXTREME OF THE PROSPERITY GOSPEL

There is no biblical guarantee of prosperity or wealth. The Bible tells us that, "the poor will always be with us" (Matthew 26:11). So, if you do not feel wealthy you are not failing. But if you have wealth 1 Timothy 6:17 gives clear counsel, "Command those who are rich in this present world not to be arrogant nor to put their hope in wealth, which is so uncertain, but to put their hope in God, who richly provides us with everything for our enjoyment."

It is important to avoid the extremes – that Christians should be poor or at the other end, which is often referred to as the prosperity gospel, that Christians should all have [great] wealth. There is a middle way, which is the stewardship gospel where we recognise that everything belongs to God.

Q: What is your perception of the prosperity gospel?

 **BIBLE ASPECTS**

6. Luke 16:13
What does this verse mean?

7. Ecclesiastes 5:10-14
What not to love or do.

8. **Colossians 3:5**
How can we do this?

VIEW POINT

1. Looking at your worldly wealth compare that to other Christians you are aware of in different countries – maybe your local church supports a particular country and people group.

2. 2How do you set your goals on achieving certain financial status or accumulating certain possessions?

3. Looking at your possessions e.g. I pad, mobile phone, do they control you or do you control your possessions?

ACTION STATIONS

1. Create two lists of those 'things' you have mind to spend money on. One list is headed 'needs' and the other 'wants'. When completed review and then compare your lists with how you feel God leading after studying the following Bible verses – Hebrews 13:5 and Philippians 4:11-13.

2. List out all that you 'own' and at the foot of the page write out, "I acknowledge that everything on this list belongs to God and that I am responsible for being a good steward."

3. If you keep a schedule of your assets the total should read, 'Total Belonging to the Lord' so even your spread sheet is aligned with the Bible!

NOTES

4. Make sure that you look after the Owner's property. Clean, tidy, well serviced

5. Be prepared to lend and don't be annoyed if it is returned in a poorer state than when it left your possession.

6. How can you make your spending decisions more spiritual? Perhaps rather asking the Lord, "how should I spend this money that you have entrusted to me?"

 **BACK TO THE BIBLE**

Here are a few additional verses that will help to deepen your understanding of what the Bible has to say about finances.

STEWARDSHIP:

1 Corinthians 4:2

Matthew 25:15; 19-21

Jeremiah 32:17

Luke 12:25-34

PROVISION:

Psalm 35:27

Joshua 1:8

Proverbs 3:9-10

Luke 12:15

1 Kings 17:4-6

Philippians 4:19

Matthew 6:33

MAN'S WISDOM

The world asks: "What does a person own? God asks, "How is the person using what they have been given?" Your use of money shows what you think of God. We will be judged on the basis of our loyalty to Christ with the time, talents, and treasures that were at our disposal.

Erwin W. Lutzer, Pastor, Moody Church

My worth to God in public is what I am in private.

Oswald Chambers

Christians cannot experience peace in the area of their finances until they have surrendered total control of this area to God and accepted their position as stewards.

Larry Burkett

LOOKING FORWARD

In our next study we will look at one topic that often comes to the forefront of the news media – debt. The Bible has a lot to say about debt but in advance of your next study it is important to know that the Bible does not preclude the believer getting into debt. But, everything the Bible does say warns about the dangers of debt and encourages the believer – and churches to become debt free.

Revisit this study and ask the Lord to help you apply what you have learnt.

Extra time

GET MORE INSIGHTS AT
→ WWW.YOURMONEYCOUNTS.ORG.UK

 ## JOIN US AT THE COFFEE SHOP

Visit www.yourmoneycounts.org.uk/blueprint-for-living for a further chance to view the coffee shop discussions related to this study.

 ## DO YOU NEED TO COMPLETE THIS STUDY?

It may be that your group did not complete this study. Why not review this study again before you next meet? There are some really important principles and personal study provides a great opportunity to weigh and pray what you have learnt and how this might apply to you.

 ## GOING DEEPER

WHAT THE BIBLE SAYS ABOUT WEALTH:

Deuteronomy 6:10-13	Can dull our spiritual vision
Deuteronomy 8:11-20	Can cause you to forget God
Nehemiah 5:9-11	Taking advantage of others to increase yours
Mark 10:21	Dealing with the love of
Mark 10:23	How it makes one less dependent on God
Luke 12:15	Not the same as the good life
Luke 12:33	Using it wisely
1 Timothy 6:17-19	Possessing much wealth carries greater responsibility

NOTES

James 1:9-11	What true wealth is
James 2:2-4	Gaining proper perspective of
Revelation 18:4-8	Can make you too comfortable

 SCRIPTURE MEMORY VERSE

A verse to commit to memory before the next study…

"The borrower is slave to the lender."

(Proverbs 22:7)

An easy verse to commit to memory. But look at the following verse – how interesting that these verses are consecutive.

 YOUR THOUGHTS, REFLECTIONS, COMMITMENTS AND ACTIONS

The Bible makes it clear that debt has always been a challenge and that it represents a serious threat to the peace of mind and freedom of the believer. The distress caused when in debt no matter how that debt has arisen causes many to lose hope. But hope is at hand and a solution does exist.

Faith and obedience play a part as does contentment and the need to be disciplined.

If you are in debt and struggling with downsizing what you owe we trust that this study will give you strength as you discover some of the biblical truths concerning debt.

———

Free to serve Him

3

SCRIPTURE MEMORY VERSE

"The borrower is slave to the lender."

Proverbs 22:7

BOUGHT

We recommend that before the next study you read a
few chapters of Bought. The relevant part for this study is:
Part 3: Free to serve Him
We suggest that you may find further help on
www.yourmoneycounts.org.uk/free-to-serve-him.

INTRODUCTION

If there is one financial term with which we are all familiar it is 'debt'. The Oxford dictionary defines debt simply as, 'a sum of money that is owed or due.' The world seeks to disguise debt seeking to make it appear less impactful than it really is. 'Buy now, pay tomorrow'. 'No payments until...' 'Consolidate your loans into one easy [lower] payment.' 'Easy terms available.' And so on. In some cases incurring debt is necessary, for example buying a house or financing student education. In other circumstances incurring debt can arise as a result of overspending, impulse purchases, an unexpected household cost or incurring costs because delaying the purchase and saving would mean that the item would not be enjoyed – now. Debt is a serious financial matter and so it is important to understand, not just the impact on our lives but also our options.

Debt can and often does give rise to worry and stress. Debt can give rise to a feeling of hopelessness. Debt can sometimes even cause people to give up. The threatening letter. Unpleasant calls.

The Bible talks about not charging usury rates. The Oxford dictionary defines usury as, 'the action or practice of lending money at unreasonably high rates of interest.' The Bible instructs us not to charge interest when lending to family, friends or the poor. (Exodus 22:25; Deuteronomy 23:19-20). The question then is what is a usury rate? There is no Biblical guideline so perhaps we could consider a household mortgage rate to be a fair rate of interest? Or maybe two to four base points above bank base rate? Good group discussion point!

THE COST OF THE CARD

The Bible sometimes uses the word 'wicked' to describe the unrighteous. In the context of debt the word may, in our opinion, be appropriated as interest rates charged by credit and store cards which have, historically, been between 15 and 30 per cent. Take a look at the following table which shows what interest the saver earns when saving £83.33 a month (£1,000 over the year) over 40 years at an interest rate 3 per cent and compares this with the interest earned by the credit card company when there is a credit

NOTES

NOTES

card debt of £5,560 with interest charged monthly at 18 per cent. In other words the credit card company is receiving £1,000 from the card holder. Please note that (2) assumes the lender makes interest at 18 per cent compounded on the £83.33 a month repayment while (3) assumes that the credit card debt remains constant at £5,560.

1. What interest would you earn with a £1,000 annual investment at 3%

Year 1	Year 10	Year 20	Year 30	Year 40
£30	£1,644	£7,357	£18,559	£37,169

2. What the lender earns from your £1,000 annual interest payment at 18 per cent

Year 1	Year 10	Year 20	Year 30	Year 40
£90	£15,638	£139,824	£832,133	£4,497,902

3. What total interest does the credit company earn on the constant card debt of £5,560?

Year 1	Year 10	Year 20	Year 30	Year 40
£1,087	£27,629	£192,558	£1,177,073	£7,053,958

Maybe this level of interest falls into the usury category!

Note: Online calculator used: thisismoney.co.uk. Different online calculators give slightly different results.

If you have credit card, store card or even a payday loan debt (even more exorbitant rates) then your faith and financial discipline has a massive role to play in downsizing your debt.

So, is the Bible silent on debt? As we will discover God has something to say and what God says we should listen to and follow.

Maybe you are not in debt. Thank the Lord for the wisdom He has given you, your faithfulness to the Word. The challenge? Continue to live debt free and be prepared to be a source of counsel to others.

FREE TO SERVE HIM

So, we understand that it is good and godly wisdom to refrain from buying stuff we cannot afford. At some point in time the day of reckoning will arise and we should be careful to avoid loading our budget up with repayments for goods and services long since used.

Q: What can we learn and apply from James 4:2?

What did you learn while growing up that has stood you in good stead today?

GAINING PERSPECTIVE

The Bible does not say that debt is sinful but every reference to debt is in the negative and attendant with warnings and an encouragement to get out of debt. Contrast that with man's economy and the easy access to credit coupled with the easy way of spending - the Internet and mobile technology have certainly transformed the ease with which we can all spend.

Don't despair. If you have debt that is causing you a problem. Be hopeful. Be prayerful. Complete this study to gain a greater understanding of what the Lord's best is for your finances. Maybe seek counsel. There is hope when your faith interacts with those areas of life that may have previously been off limits. You have not failed. Maybe you could have done things differently? Yes, you and the rest of us. The Lord has open arms, He knows and understands everything and there is nothing off limits that He cannot reach into.

DEBT MAY DENY GOD AN OPPORTUNITY:

When we incur debt we may deny God an opportunity. The Lord may wish us to pray in order that He may provide. How about saving and waiting for the time when that purchase can be made? How much 'stuff' have you bought that you never really use? There are so many storage facilities where people can store stuff. Websites that enable us to give away possessions that we no longer use. And, if you save it is possible that the need or desire for that item may diminish to the point where it is no longer on your 'to buy' list.

NOTES

NOTES

DEBT PRESUMES:

So often we borrow to the hilt thinking that our finances will continue as they are. But what about the possibility of a job loss? Or ill health? Debt always presumes on the future.

YOUR HOUSEHOLD MORTGAGE

Does the Bible speak against a household mortgage? Consider this – you may choose to agree, or not. When renting you sign up to make monthly payments and incur a regular financial commitment. When you take out a mortgage you similarly sign up to a monthly commitment. But, if you default on the rent or mortgage payment – then you are in arrears – and in debt. The key surely is not to borrow more than you can afford, not to borrow more than you can repay should interest rates rise by, say, 2 per cent. When you move make sure that you do not extend the mortgage back to 25 or 30 years. Why not reduce the outstanding term by a couple of years?

STUDENT DEBT

Free education might have been enjoyed by many but not today's students. Parents may be able to help. Some study at local universities and remain home based. Some students work to minimise debt. Some refrain from the more costly nature of university life. That said, it is still a burden of debt on people at the start of their adult lives. There is the danger that it creates in young people a culture and acceptance of debt, an acceptance that focuses on 'living up to the max.'

DOWNSIZING DEBT

Visit www.yourmoneycounts.org.uk for the keys to downsizing your debt, avoiding the car debt trap and much much more.

Q: What are you learning about debt that is especially helpful?

THE PRACTICAL SOLUTION

Maybe you are in debt and you find yourself encouraged that God has included wisdom in the Bible that directly relates to the situation in which you find yourself. Maybe, apart from possibly your home loan you do not find yourself in debt – a situation for which you give thanks and also perhaps you further resolve to stay debt free.

Your first step should be to continue the journey of seeking the Lord. He does not condemn anyone for having taken what might perhaps be unwise decisions. As our heavenly Father He is committed to all those who love Him. But downsizing debt can be like losing weight in that it takes time, resolve, effort and perseverance. So first step, trust the Lord and pray. Pray and apply how you sense Romans 13:8 applies to your situation.

What practical steps could you or should you take? While our study together is not the setting for debt management or reduction the website www.yourmoneycounts.org.uk provides further help and guidance. However, as a take away and first step in getting to grips with debt it is important to address the causes of the debt. Debt may have arisen because of your circumstances - a lost job or perhaps a consequence of a relationship breakdown. Somehow you must work toward making ends meet and living within income. Easy to read but not always easy to put into practice. But every journey has to start somewhere. Taking the decision not to make purchases unless the money is available. This means saying 'no' when the impulses to buy are strong. Ask the Lord to help you be more content by thanking Him for those things that you already have.

Be drastic with the plastic. Cut up those cards where the account is not under your control.

Do you need to seek godly counsel?

ADVICE AND COUNSEL

Two attitudes keep us from seeking counsel. The first is pride and the second stubbornness. But the Lord encourages us to seek godly counsel.

WHAT DO WE LEARN FROM?

Proverbs 12:15

Proverbs 15:22

NOTES

NOTES

Proverbs 19:20

Psalm 119:24

Hebrews 4:12

Proverbs 6:20-22

 ## BIBLE ASPECTS

Read and consider what you can learn from...

1.   Proverbs 22:7
How does the Bible contrast the one who is in debt?

2.   Romans 13:8
What does Paul encourage us to do?

3.   1 Corinthians 7:23
What do we become when in debt?

4.   Galatians 5:1
How are we called to live life?

5. **James 4:13-17**
What is one of debt's traps?

6. **Psalm 37:21**
Do not fail to repay.

7. **2 Kings 4:1-7**
What principles of getting out of debt can you identify from this passage? How might these apply today?

VIEW POINT

1. What was new to you?
2. What was of most interest from the study that was particularly helpful?
3. How do you feel about how easy it is to access credit?
4. What do you think about the true long-term cost of card debt?
5. How would it feel to have no debt of any kind?
6. What can we learn about guaranteeing debts from Proverbs 6:1-5 and 17:18?
7. What are the benefits of seeking counsel?
8. What are some of the benefits you have experienced from seeking counsel?

NOTES

NOTES

 **ACTION STATIONS**

If you are a slave to man through debt, other people control your decisions. The key is to get out of debt so that you can better follow how the Bible directs and make the choices that He desires for you to make instead of what man desires.

REASONS TO GET OUT OF DEBT

1. Because God's Word encourages us to do so
2. Getting out of debt helps us to prepare for financial uncertainties in the future
3. Getting out of debt helps us prepare for retirement
4. Getting out of debt saves us a lot of money
5. Getting out of debt can free us up to do God's Will
6. Because debt that we can "afford now" can give rise to problems in the future.

A FEW KEYS TO HELP YOU STAY OUT OF DEBT

1. Grow your emergency fund
2. Make smart purchasing decisions
3. Plan present and future expenses
4. Adopt a debt-free lifestyle
5. Keep accurate records
6. Stop using credit
7. Adhere to your spending plan.

Take control – Well, all things considered that is what the solution is all about. It's about making informed choices about what is right for you and your loved ones.

BACK TO THE BIBLE

Here are a few additional verses that will help to deepen your understanding of what the Bible has to say about finances.

- Deuteronomy 15:7-8
- Deuteronomy 15:1-3
- Deuteronomy 28
- Proverbs 3:27-28
- Proverbs 17:18
- Proverbs 22:26-27
- Proverbs 27:1
- Isaiah 32:17

NOTES

NOTES

MAN'S WISDOM

No investment is as secure as a repaid debt.

Finnish Proverb

God opposes usury and greed, yet no one realises this because it is not murder or robbery.

Martin Luther, Theologian, 1483-1546

Often all it takes to start down the road to bankruptcy is an increase in income.

Mark Lloydbottom

LOOKING FORWARD

Our next study looks at the subject of giving. This is a subject that many church leaders are uncomfortable teaching and one that those listening sometimes prefer not to hear. Let's look afresh at what the Bible imparts about an area of our Christian faith that is really important.
Although giving can be challenging at times, the potential benefits to the giver make it one of the most exciting and fulfilling areas of our entire Christian life.

Revisit this study and ask the Lord to help you apply hat you have learnt.

Extra time

GET MORE INSIGHTS AT
→ WWW.YOURMONEYCOUNTS.ORG.UK

NOTES

 ## JOIN US AT THE COFFEE SHOP

Visit www.yourmoneycounts.org.uk/free-to-serve-him for a further chance to view the coffee shop discussions related to this study.

 ## DO YOU NEED TO COMPLETE THIS STUDY?

It may be that your group did not complete this study. Why not review this study again before you next meet? There are some really important principles and personal study provides a great opportunity to weigh and pray what you have learnt and how this might apply to you.

 ## PARENTS

Teaching your children about managing the money that passes through their hands and how they manage cards and the easy invitation to swipe and buy is important. We will look further at this in a later study but for now you might like to look at our Parent Money Management Questionnaire.

PARENT MONEY MANAGEMENT QUESTIONNAIRE

This questionnaire is designed to help parents focus on some of the aspects of money education for your children. There is no right or wrong answer. The purpose of the questions is to stir up your thinking about certain attitudes and behaviour. The questions relate to two specific areas of financial concern: your children's money and their possessions.

T F 1. I consistently give into my child's demands for more things, whether I think he or she has earned them or not.

T F 2. I give my child a regular allowance and allow him or her to decide how to budget and spend it.

T F   3. My child's room is filled almost to overflowing with toys and other fun things, largely because my neighbour's children have the same.

T F   4. I periodically require my child to list and evaluate his or her possessions to determine their present practicality and usefulness.

Good parenting tip. Teach your children what the Bible says about the handling of money and possessions. Show and practice the ways of the Lord (Proverbs 22:6) before the world teaches them (how to spend, spend, oh and borrow as well).

Under 7s   – Give Save Spend

8-12s   – The Secret

Teens   – Two Masters

Order copies of these books from: www.yourmoneycounts.org.uk/shop

SCRIPTURE MEMORY VERSE

A verse to commit to memory before the next study…

"Remember the words of the Lord Jesus that He said that 'it is more blessed to give than receive'."

(Acts 20:35)

YOUR THOUGHTS, REFLECTIONS, COMMITMENTS AND ACTIONS

There is one very clear difference between the world's approach to finances and God's. That is intentional generosity. Giving is a godly command. It helps us outwork God's plan that our faith should not be in our bank balance but in Him. The act of giving is one way that we tell ourselves we have enough.

Giving is not God's way of raising money. It's God's way of raising people into the likeness of His Son.

In looking at generosity it is important to remember that God owns everything, and it is more blessed to give than to receive.

Growing in generosity

4

SCRIPTURE MEMORY VERSE

"Remember the words of the Lord Jesus that He said that 'it is more blessed to give than receive'"

Acts 20:35

BOUGHT

We recommend that before the next study you read a few chapters of Bought. The relevant part for this study is:
Part 4: Growing in generosity.
You may also wish to visit:
www.yourmoneycounts.org.uk/growing-in-generosity.

INTRODUCTION

For most giving is still an unnatural act. The prevailing attitude is that 'what is mine is mine' and that to give is to deny the opportunity of spending, or perhaps saving. We give generously to the annual televised charity appeals – about £1.50 for every UK adult. But do we give generously as the Bible prescribes is the habit of one who loves the Lord? Giving is one of those subjects that preachers most talk about when it comes to money. Not just because the Church needs income, but more importantly because giving is an instruction from the Lord. One preacher said to his congregation as his pre offering talk, "Would you like the good news or the bad news?" He then told them that, "the good news is that the Church has a fully funded budget for the next year. The bad news is that all the money is in your pockets."

Yet few areas of the Christian life can be more misunderstood and frustrating than that of giving. Who doesn't sense the loss of that which is given? It is after all money that could so easily be used to buy something. What is the personal gain of giving away? We will explore what the Bible has to say and engage with how God seeks to direct us so that we are transformed by the renewing of our minds rather than conformed to the ways of the world – the [fleshly] desires of our minds.

For many years after I accepted Christ, even after I was married, I understood little of the importance of giving. In my early years I would see the offering plate handed around. I could see that the plate had to bear the weight of coins although occasionally a note or two fluttered around. Today I sometimes count the Church offering and still see many small coins although there are many more cheques and notes.

ATTITUDE IN GIVING

God evaluates our actions on the basis of our attitudes. John 3:16 reveals His attitude toward giving: "for God so loved the world that He gave us His one and only Son." Because God loved, He gave. Because God is love, He is also a giver. He set the example of giving motivated by love.

NOTES

In God's economy, the attitude is more important than the amount. Jesus emphasised this in Matthew 23:23: "Woe to you, teachers of the law and Pharisees, you hypocrites! You give a tenth of your spices – mint, dill and cumin. But you have neglected the more important matters of the law – justice, mercy and faithfulness. You should have practiced the latter, without neglecting the former."

In addition to giving with love, we are called to give cheerfully. "Each of you should give what you have decided in your heart to give, not reluctantly or under compulsion, for God loves a cheerful giver" 2 Corinthians 9:7. The original Greek word for cheerful is hilarious, which is translated into the English word hilarious. We are to be joyful givers.

When was the last time you saw hilarity when the offering plate passed? The atmosphere more often reminds us of a patient in the dentist chair awaiting a painful extraction. So, how to develop hilarity in our giving? Consider the Macedonian churches: "we want you to know about the grace that God has given the Macedonian churches. In the midst of a very severe trial, their overflowing joy and their extreme poverty welled up in rich generosity" (2 Corinthians 8:1-2).

How did the Macedonians, who were in terrible circumstances, 'severe trial' and 'extreme poverty,' still manage to give with 'overflowing joy?' The answer is in verse five: "they gave themselves first to the Lord and then to us in keeping with God's will." The key to cheerful giving is to yield ourselves to Christ and ask Him to direct how much He wants us to give.

Q: What attitudes should characterise our giving?

THE AMOUNT TO GIVE

In Scripture we find three types of giving. [1] The tithe. [2] Freewill offering. [3] Gifts to the poor. But how much should we give?

Before the Old Testament Law, there were two instances of giving a known amount. In Genesis 14:20, Abraham gave 10 per cent – a tithe - after the rescue of his nephew Lot. And in Genesis 28:22, Jacob promised to give a tenth of all his possessions if God brought him safely through his journey.

With the Law came the requirement to tithe. The Lord condemns the children of Israel in Malachi 3:8-9 for not tithing properly: "will a man rob God? Yet you rob me. But you ask, 'How do we rob you?' In tithes and offerings. You are under a curse – the whole nation of you –because you are robbing me!'"

God also made another significant provision for the poor in Deuteronomy 15:7-8: "If anyone is poor among your fellow Israelites in any of the towns of the land that the Lord your God is giving you, do not be hard-hearted or tight-fisted towards them. Rather, be open-handed and freely lend them whatever they need." Even under the law, the extent of one's giving was not to be limited by a fixed percentage but was to be adjusted by surrounding needs.

The New Testament teaches that we are to give in proportion: "On the first day of every week, each one of you should set aside a sum of money in keeping with your income, saving it up, so that when I come no collections will have to be made" 1 Corinthians 16:2.

How much to give? That is for you to weigh what the Word instructs us to do and then to commit and action. One thing is certain that we cannot outgive God. One pastor told his congregation one Sunday that, "you are never more like Jesus than when you are giving." Bernard Edinger, a French Jewish journalist once said: "The world will never be won to Christ with what people can conveniently spare. While John Wesley said, "Money never stays with me. It would burn me if it did. I throw it out of my hands as soon as possible, lest it should finds its way into my heart.

THE HUMAN RESPONSE

For many giving does not come naturally. Even as an author of books and studies on biblical finance I still find that giving is not one of my natural habits. It is a discipline, a recurring habit, a commitment as well as a joy and responding to the nature and character of the Lord Jesus Christ.

We all spend time planning what to do at Christmas, where to go and what to do when we have a holiday. Maybe you, like so many others plan to spend time watching television. But, how much time do we spend planning our finances and in particular where does our giving plan come into this?

NOTES

NOTES

A few years ago I was on a church mission trip in a West African country. I was invited to attend a Church and as I was accompanying the visiting speaker I was invited to sit on the front row. When it came to the offering everyone was required to file down to the front and place their offering in one of two offering baskets. As I watched from the corner of my eye I could see that some dropped in what looked like the smallest of currencies while others had no money but just put their hands in and out. How did I feel? Sorry. Sorry to be so close to so many poor people. But poor people who loved the Lord. My point? In the western world and especially in the UK we are an island of plenty surrounded by a world in need. Let us not neglect to give all that we can and invest into countries where there is such need.

We all have choices with regard to how we handle the money that comes through our hands. It is important to plan and be intentional about the handling of our finances so that we can be free to give. We are, after all called to be wise stewards and our giving is a demonstration and response to our faith in our loving heavenly Father.

Q: Does God really want your money? What does He want more than your money?

BIBLE ASPECTS

Read and consider what you can learn from...

1. 1 Corinthians 13:3

What does this passage communicate about the importance of proper attitude in giving?

2. **Luke 12:34**
What is one benefit from giving?

3. **1 Timothy 6:18-19**
And another benefit?

4. **Galatians 2:9-10**
What do we learn about our giving to the poor?

5. **Matthew 25:35-45**
How does Jesus identify with the needy and how does this affect your thinking?

6. **Numbers 18:8-10**
What do these verses tell you about financially supporting your church?

NOTES

NOTES

VIEW POINT

1. Do you feel led to make any change to your planned giving?
2. Do you have a commitment to tithing?
3. How do you feel toward giving to the poor?

ACTION STATIONS

1. Why should you give?
2. How should you give?
3. How do you feel about your current level of giving?
4. How do you feel about creating a giving plan?
5. Could you include one poor person in your giving plan?

BACK TO THE BIBLE

Here are a few additional verses that will help to deepen your understanding of what the Bible has to say about giving.

Mathew 6:4

2 Corinthians 9:6-11

John 3:16

Proverbs 3:5-10

Acts 4:32

MAN'S WISDOM

You're never more like Jesus than when you are giving.

Pastor Johnny Hunt

He who bestows his goods upon the poor shall have as much again and ten times more.

John Bunyan, Preacher

God has given us two hands, one to receive and the other to give.

Billy Graham

LOOKING FORWARD

One of the barriers that some express is a lack of residual income after personal and household costs have been met. Perhaps the importance attached to giving in the Bible might compel a change in the approach to your finances. Giving should be on the first line item on our budgets in order to avoid being in a situation whereby you feel you cannot afford to give or what you give is short of what you feel called to give.

Revisit this study and ask the Lord to help you apply what you have learnt.

Extra time

GET MORE INSIGHTS AT
→ WWW.YOURMONEYCOUNTS.ORG.UK

 JOIN US AT THE COFFEE SHOP

Visit www.yourmoneycounts.org.uk/resources for a further chance to view the coffee shop discussions related to this study.

 DO YOU NEED TO COMPLETE THIS STUDY?

It may be that your group did not complete this study. Why not review this study again before you next meet? There are some really important principles and personal study provides a great opportunity to weigh and pray what you have learnt and how this might apply to you.

 GOING DEEPER

NEW TESTAMENT GUIDELINES FOR GIVING: GIVE, CHRISTIAN GIVE

There are no exceptions. "Each man should give what he has decided in his head to give." 2 Corinthians 9:7

Mark 14:3-9	Give generously
1 Corinthians 16:2 2 Corinthians 8:8-11	Give regularly and systematically
2 Corinthians 8:4; 9:7	Give voluntarily
2 Corinthians 8:2 Acts 20:35 Matthew 6:21	Give joyfully
Acts 10:1-4 2 Corinthians 8:9 Matthew 25:40 Matthew 5:23, 24	Give worshipfully

NOTES

Acts 11:29 1 Corinthians 16:2 Mark 12:43-44	Give proportionately
2 Corinthians 8:3 Luke 21:1-4 2 Samuel 24:24	Give sacrificially
Matthew 6:1-4	Give quietly

THE LORD'S PROVISION FOR THE GIVER

In Proverbs 11:24-25 and in Luke 6:38, the Bible makes it clear that in many cases God blesses us financially when we give generously and in 2 Corinthians 9:6, God reminds us that the sower who sows little or no seed will receive little or possibly none. However, the sower who sows generously will reap generously. God prospers us not just so we can have more ourselves, but that we can give even more to those who are in need. 2 Corinthians 9:11 – God's extra provision is usually not intended to raise our standard of living but to raise our standard of giving.

 ### SCRIPTURE MEMORY VERSES

A verse to commit to memory before the next study on:

Saving: "Steady plodding brings prosperity; hasty speculation brings poverty."

(Proverbs 21:5)

Spending: "I have learned to be content in whatever circumstances I am. I know how to get along with humble means, and I also know how to live in prosperity...I can do all things through Him who strengthens me."

(Philippians 4:11-13)

YOUR THOUGHTS, REFLECTIONS, COMMITMENTS AND ACTIONS

NOTES

With so many transactions being made by card, and increasingly by swipe, keeping track of those card and bank balances is not always easy. If our finances are going to be ordered so that they are handled in a sound and godly manner it is important to have a plan that you follow and adhere to so far as possible. Being intentional is essential if our finances are to be a source of blessing instead of something of a nightmare and worry.

We trust that as you complete this final Money or Maker study that this has been of real help to you. This, together with Bought have provided an overview of some of the main principles in the 2350 Bible verses regarding the handling of money and possessions.

———

Save.
Invest.
Spend.

5

SCRIPTURE MEMORY VERSES

Save/Invest: "Steady plodding brings prosperity; hasty speculation brings poverty"

Acts 20:35

Spend: "I have learned to be content in whatever circumstances I am. I know how to get along with humble means, and I also know how to live in prosperity… I can do all things through Him who strengthens me."

Philippians 4:11-13

BOUGHT

We recommend that before the final study you read a few chapters of Bought. The relevant part for this study is:
Part 5: Save. Invest. Spend.
Also visit www.yourmoneycounts.org.uk/save-invest-spend

INTRODUCTION

Managing our financial resources involves balancing what we receive with what we spend. The key to financial success is to ensure that spending is less than our income and that we save regularly over a long period of time. Well of course that is easy to read but maybe not so easy to put into practice especially as your finances will already have an established pattern and commitments. Expenditure may currently exceed income while consumer and card debts may be a cause for concern. Does the Bible have anything to say about our spending and saving?

During the years leading up the 2008 global financial crisis, debt – both personal and government spiraled. During the four or five subsequent years personal consumer debt reduced only to start increasing when many perceived that the economy was improving. This is not an unfamiliar financial pattern. When the economy is perceived as being buoyant spending and debt increase only for the rubber to hit the road as inevitably it does. Contrast that with Joseph's interpretation of Potiphar's dream (Genesis 41:17-30; 33-36). Joseph interpreted Potiphar's dream and was then instrumental in everyone saving during the seven good years in preparation for the seven lean years.

It is important not to overcommit financially or to omit giving and saving. Yielding to the temptations of the 'have it and have it now because you deserve it' culture is important if we are to avoid falling into the traps of man's economy.

Creating a carefully prepared spending plan that takes into account the fact that some costs occur throughout the year such as insurances, Christmas and birthday presents, car costs and so on. These 'periodic costs' need to be identified and funds set aside each month so that the money is there when the bills arise.

God calls us to be wise stewards and having a spending plan that has income greater than expenditure is a wise plan that represents a first step toward being in control of your finances. The next step is keeping to the plan – and that often means reigning in 'impulse' spending. This step outworks the principle that spending decisions are also spiritual decisions.

NOTES

NOTES

SAVING

Paul tells Timothy in 1 Timothy 6:10 that "the love of money is a [not the] root of all sorts of evil." It is not money itself but the wrong attitude toward money that is the root of much evil.

The Bible is clear that we should not seek to be hoarders. Why? The challenge is seen in Matthew 6:19-21 where Matthew tells us we should not put store in treasures and wealth on earth because nothing is secure. When we do we face the danger that our heart follows that which we treasure.

Jesus makes it clear in the parable of the rich man (Luke 12:16-21, 34) where the key is the word 'all.' Jesus called the rich man a fool because he saved all of his goods. He stored them up for his own use. He did not balance his saving with generous giving. We should save and invest only when we also are giving to the Lord. Why? The answer can be found in Mathew 6:21 "Where your treasure is, there your heart will be also."

THERE ARE TWO TYPES OF SAVING:

Short term: This saving is for unexpected costs, e.g. to replace a household appliance or to pay for something such as a new computer. These savings are also there to cover emergencies such as loss of job, an illness or other interruption of income. How much? That depends – why not discuss this within your small group? Our answer is that maybe somewhere from one month to six month's income.

Long term: This saving is intended to fund long-term needs such as retirement income. Proverbs 21:20 tells us that "the wise man saves for the future, but the foolish man spends whatever he gets."

Proverbs 21:5 gives an insight into the importance of saving regularly over a long period of time. Even in times of low returns your capital will grow over time.

The fundamental principle to being a successful investor is to spend less than you earn. Then save and invest the difference over a long period of time.

OTHER BIBLICAL POINTERS

Avoid risky investments. Ecclesiastes 5:13-15 talks about speculating "There is another serious problem I have seen everywhere

– savings are put into risky investments that turn sour, and soon there is nothing left to pass on to one's son. The man who speculates soon returns to where he began – with nothing."

The lesson? Avoid get rich quick schemes. Avoid being pressured into making hasty decisions. Be very wary of high profit or high interest rates that are 'practically guaranteed.'

Diversify. Ecclesiastes 11:2 tells us to "divide your portion to seven, or eight, for you do not know what misfortune may occur on the earth." Spread your investment portfolio.

Q: How can saving help alleviate stress and head off potential problems?

SPENDING

Do you have a spending plan? That is the term we prefer to use rather than the word budget, which conjures up the idea of a rather technical exercise that never seems to work out how it should.

Man's economy is committed to helping you make spending decisions and, if you don't have enough money, then there is a solution on hand – debt.

While so much of expenditure seems to be unavoidable it is surprising how much the pressures of the world have turned discretionary expenditure into compulsory expenditure. For example, mobile phones, satellite television, new technology costs all appear to fit into this category. Even today we do not have satellite TV – that is not just a cost decision it is also one based on not wishing to spend time in front of a TV screen all the time.

Q: What costs do you think we incur that could fit into this category?

The apostle Paul, the author of about two thirds of the New Testament has the answer and it is found in 1 Timothy 6:8 "if we have food and covering we will be content with that." And also in Philippians 4:11-13 "I am not saying this because I am in need, for I have learned to be content whatever the circumstances. I know what it is to be in need, and I know what it is to have plenty. I have learned

NOTES

NOTES

the secret of being content in any and every situation, whether well fed or hungry, whether living in plenty or in want. I can do everything through Him who gives me strength."

Controlling the impulses of the mind or the desires of the heart and aligning your thinking with Paul's will help control some of those spending desires. When we see something we would like we practice the discipline of having a look at the available options before returning home and allowing those 'must have' impulses to ebb away. That is not to say that we never return to make a purchase but often that is the case. One time a missionary stayed at our home for two weeks while we were away and the first thing he said was how peaceful the home was and how little there was in it. That is a whole lot easier when there are not young children around!

Q: How can we develop a greater inner sense of contentment?

Spending plan: www.yourmoneycounts.org.uk/resources/workbooks

Motorists are accustomed to using a satnav to aid navigation. And most households have plans for such events as holidays and Christmas. Creating a spending plan is essential. Bought and the yourmoneycounts.org website contain a lot of helpful information.

Q: Discuss ideas that work for creating a balanced spending plan – and how to keep to it

BENEFITS OF A SPENDING PLAN

1. Financial freedom
2. Can act to bring the family together
3. Gives you a sense of peace about your finances
4. Helps you establish what is really important in your life
5. Gives you a taste of financial success regardless of your income level
6. Improves your self confidence

7. Helps you to be a smarter consumer
8. Helps you to enjoy the extra money that you save or make
9. Frees you up to provide for your family and do the will of the Lord
10. Instead of borrowing money you can trim your spending and have money to pay cash for the things you wish to buy
11. Helps you to better control your spending.

DEVELOPING A SPENDING PLAN

1. Identify how your money is currently spent penny by penny over a 30-day period
2. Then, develop a spending plan based on your values, necessities and goals. This should take into account your personal and household needs, your giving commitment and future needs.
3. Track your spending and stay in line with your plan.

HOW TO STAY IN LINE WITH YOUR PLAN

1. Make giving to God a priority
2. Make sure your budget is not too constrictive or too loose
3. Make sure that you allow money for unplanned expenses and an emergency fund
4. Track your spending and manage your spending plan
5. Keep track of your spending daily
6. Make necessary adjustments but be careful not to adjust your budget for impulse purchases
7. Watch out for cash machine or supermarket 'cash-back' temptations
8. Realise that the pain of following a spending plan comes mostly at the beginning.

NOTES

NOTES

OTHER TIPS:

1. Beware of luxuries dressed as necessities
2. Don't raise your standard of living every time you receive a pay rise
3. Have fun within your means
4. If married, work on your spending plan together
5. If you are married, develop an amount that you or your spouse can spend without checking with the other one
6. Realise that adjusting your spending habits is a process – allow yourself time to adjust
7. Adopt an attitude that every penny is important.

Remember Proverbs 13:11…"he who gathers money little by little makes it grow."

 **BIBLE ASPECTS**

Read and consider what you can learn from…

1. Genesis 41:34-36
What does this passage say about savings?

2. Luke 12:16-21, 34
Why did the Lord call the rich man a fool?

3. **1 Timothy 6:9-10**
According to these verses, why is it wrong to want to get rich?

4. **Philippians 4:11-13**
What do these verses say about contentment?

5. **Acts 4:32-37**
What do these verses have in common?

VIEW POINT

1. What saving experiences can you share that you think might be a help to others?

2. What cost saving habits do you have that might be insightful for others?

3. What are the advantages of having a spending plan and keeping to it?

4. Should Christians always prosper financially?

5. What influence do adverts, banner ads, magazines, catalogues and other advertisements have on your spending and lifestyle?

6. Do you sense that the Lord would have you change your spending or your standard of living?

7. If you have children, how will you train them to manage their finances wisely?

NOTES

 **ACTION STATIONS**

1. Do you have a savings plan that will enable you to cover any unexpected costs? (Short to medium term planning)

2. Do you have an investment plan that will enable you to be financially independent in your latter years? (Long term planning)

3. Can you reduce your expenses that will enable you to give and/or save more?

 **BACK TO THE BIBLE**

Here are a few additional verses that will help to deepen your understanding of what the Bible has to say about saving and spending.

> Philippians 4:19
>
> Proverbs 21:5
>
> James 1:17
>
> Luke 16:10
>
> 1 Timothy 5:8
>
> Matthew 6:21

MAN'S WISDOM

Losses from unwise investments seem even more common in the Christian community than outside it.

Randy Alcorn

Spend less than you earn and do it for a long time and you will be financially successful.

Ron Blue, Kingdom Advisors

GOING FORWARD

How do you find your thoughts, attitudes and plans have changed now you are nearing the end of Money or Maker? You will not be the first if you feel that these studies have opened your eyes to the wonder and relevance of God's Word in this area of our lives. We have looked at how we handle our money impacts our fellowship with the Lord and how money is one of the primary competitors with Christ for the lordship of our life, and money also molds our characters.

Now you have begun the journey of getting to grips with the 7 per cent of the Bible that shows how God's economy works why not continue? Our website yourmoneycounts.org.uk has a range of books for children, teenagers and business owners. We encourage you to visit our website and look at our resources for children, teens and business owners

Revisit this study and ask the Lord to help you apply what you have learnt.

Extra time

GET MORE INSIGHTS AT
→ WWW.YOURMONEYCOUNTS.ORG.UK

 JOIN US AT THE COFFEE SHOP

Visit www.yourmoneycounts.org.uk/resources yourmoneycounts.org for a further chance to view the coffee shop discussions related to this study.

 DO YOU NEED TO COMPLETE THIS STUDY?

It may be that your group did not complete this study. Why not review this study again before you next meet? There are some really important principles and personal study provides a great opportunity to weigh and pray what you have learnt and how this might apply to you.

 GOING DEEPER

BOUGHT

We recommend that after studying Money or Maker you read the final chapter in: Part 6: Summing it all up.

As this is your own personal study book why not prepare a record of all that you have learnt. The decisions and commitments you have made. Applying biblical financial principles is a journey that takes time. It's easy to become discouraged when your finances aren't completely under control by the end of this study. It takes the average person a year to apply most of these principles, and even longer if you have made financial mistakes.

Some people become frustrated by the inability to solve their financial problems quickly. Remember simply be faithful with what you have – be it little or much. Some abandon the goal of becoming debt-free or increasing their saving or giving because the task looks impossible. And perhaps it is – without the Lord's help. Your role is to make a genuine effort, no matter how small it may appear, and then leave the results to God. I love what the Lord said to the

NOTES

prophet Zechariah, "For who has despised the day of small things" (Zechariah 4:10). Don't be discouraged. Be persistent. Be faithful in even the smallest matters. We have repeatedly seen the Lord bless those who tried to be faithful.

We appreciate the effort you have invested in this study. And we pray this has given you a greater appreciation for the Bible, helped close friendships, and above all, nurtured your love for Jesus Christ. May the Lord richly bless you on your journey to true financial freedom.

A SIXTH STUDY MEETING?

Before leaving the subject of money and finance God's way why not hold a social at your next meeting and have everyone bring something to eat. Then have a time of feedback, and sharing how the Lord is leading you and praying for one another.

YOUR THOUGHTS, REFLECTIONS, COMMITMENTS AND ACTIONS

"Everything in the heavens and earth is yours, O Lord, and this is your kingdom. We adore you as being in control of everything. Riches and honour come from you alone, and you are the ruler of all mankind; your hand controls power and might, and it is at your discretion that men are made great and given strength."

1 Chronicles 29:11-12

www.ingramcontent.com/pod-product-compliance
Lightning Source LLC
Chambersburg PA
CBHW042036100526
44587CB00030B/4445